Guide Dogs

by

Charles and Linda George

Content Consultant:
Carol Lippert Gray
Manager of Public Relations
The Seeing Eye

190984717

CAPSTONE BOOKS

an imprint of Capstone Press
Mankato, Minnesota

Capstone Books are published by Capstone Press
151 Good Counsel Drive, P.O. Box 669, Mankato, Minnesota 56002
http://www.capstone-press.com

Printed in the United States of America.

Library of Congress Cataloging-in-Publication Data
George, Charles, 1949-
    Guide dogs/by Charles and Linda George.
    p. cm.--(Dogs at work)
    Includes bibliographical references (p. 45) and index.
    Summary: Describes the selection, training, accomplishments, and
history of guide dogs.
    ISBN 1-56065-754-5
    1. Guide dogs--United States--Juvenile literature. [1. Guide dogs.]
I. George, Linda. II. Title. III. Series.
HV1780.G46   1998
636.7'088'6--dc21

                                          97-31741
                                            CIP
                                            AC

Editorial credits:
Editor, Christy Steele; cover design, James Franklin; photo research,
    Michelle L. Norstad

Photo credits:
Peter Byron, 40
David Macias, 14, 16, 18, 20, 23, 24, 37
The Seeing Eye, 7, 8, 11, 38, 41
Unicorn Stock Photos, 4; H.H. Thomas, 13; Florent Flipper, cover, 27,
    29, 30, 33, 34, 43

Table of Contents

History of Guide Dogs

Guide dogs lead people who cannot see well. They guide people through the everyday world. The dogs stop for objects like curbs or stairs. They lead their masters around obstacles. An obstacle is an object that gets in the way.

Obstacles can be on the ground. For example, guide dogs lead their masters around fences, bars, or holes in the ground. Obstacles can be in the air, too. For example, guide dogs stop their masters from walking into hanging tree branches.

First Guide Dogs

Dogs have guided people for hundreds of years. No one knows who decided to train dogs

Guide dogs lead their masters around obstacles.

as guides. In the 1600s, a famous artist named Rembrandt painted blind men and their guide dogs. At the time, blind people who wanted guide dogs had to train the dogs themselves. Training programs did not exist.

Things did not change until World War I (1914-1918). In 1916, the German Army began a guide-dog training program. The Germans trained German shepherd dogs to guide people. They gave these dogs to German soldiers who lost their sight during the war.

Some North Americans heard about Germany's success with guide dogs. But they did not begin training guide dogs. Most people felt that German shepherds would be too fierce to guide people.

Dorothy Eustis

Dorothy Eustis was an American who lived in Switzerland after World War I. She was a dog breeder. She saw how much guide dogs helped people. In 1927, Eustis wrote an article about

Dorothy Eustis was a dog breeder. She saw how much guide dogs helped people.

guide dogs for the magazine *The Saturday Evening Post.*

Eustis received hundreds of letters after her article was printed. The letters came from blind people in the United States. Most of the people wanted to know how to get guide dogs.

One of the letters was from a blind man named Morris Frank. Two childhood accidents caused Frank to lose his sight. Frank wanted Eustis to teach him how to use a guide dog. In return, Frank promised he would show other people how helpful guide dogs could be.

Eustis liked Morris Frank's letter. Eustis selected a dog to train as his guide and invited Frank to Switzerland.

Eustis trained a female guide dog named Buddy. Buddy changed Frank's life. Frank was able to go places he could not go before.

Buddy changed Frank's life. Frank was able to go places he could not go before.

Frank and Buddy

Frank and Buddy returned to the United States. They traveled all over the country. Frank wanted other people to see how well a dog could guide a blind person. People were amazed that Buddy could guide Frank through busy streets. Newspapers wrote stories about them. Buddy and Frank became famous.

Buddy proved to North Americans that dogs could guide people. People began to accept guide dogs. Soon restaurant owners, bus drivers, and train conductors let Buddy come inside with Frank.

Buddy rescued Frank many times during her life. She pulled Frank away from running horses and fast cars. Buddy helped Frank escape from a burning hotel.

She even saved Frank from drowning. Frank became tired while he was swimming one day. Buddy jumped in the water and swam to Frank. Frank put his arms around Buddy's neck and she swam to shore.

Dorothy Eustis started The Seeing Eye school in 1929. This is the school's first graduating class.

Buddy died when she was 12 years old. People from around the world sent Frank letters praising Buddy.

Schools for Guide Dogs

Frank and Buddy made the idea of guide dogs popular in North America. Many more people wanted guide dogs. In 1929, Dorothy Eustis founded The Seeing Eye in Tennessee. The Seeing Eye is a school that trains guide dogs. Today, the school is in Morristown, New Jersey. Dogs that train there are called Seeing Eye® dogs.

The Seeing Eye received many requests for guide dogs. The school could not provide a dog for every person who wanted one. More schools started training guide dogs. Today, there are about 14 schools in North America that train guide dogs.

Today, there are about 14 schools in North America that train guide dogs.

Best Breeds

Guide dogs have certain qualities. They are smart, willing to learn, and anxious to please. Guide dogs are not afraid of people or unknown places. The dogs respond well to praise. They need to ignore distractions like noise or cats and keep working.

Guide dogs should be 20 to 28 inches (51 to 71 centimeters) tall at their shoulders. Larger dogs may not fit into cars. They may also be too big to fit under tables. Smaller dogs have a hard time keeping up with people.

Guide dogs must be in good physical condition to handle their active lives. They guide owners up and down stairs. They go on

Guide dogs should be small enough to fit under tables.

Many guide dogs are Labrador retrievers.

long walks. They must be strong enough to pull their owners away from danger.

Many breeds make ideal guide dogs. These breeds include collies, Australian shepherds, and boxers. But German shepherds, Labrador retrievers, and golden retrievers are the three most popular breeds.

German Shepherds

German shepherds were the first breed trained as guide dogs. Trainers chose German shepherds because of their strong, muscular bodies.

German shepherds have the right build to be guide dogs. They grow 22 to 26 inches (56 to 66 centimeters) tall. They weigh 55 to 95 pounds (25 to 43 kilograms).

German shepherds are suited for guiding people in all types of weather. Their thick coats keep them warm and dry.

Labrador Retrievers

Labrador retrievers are named after the Labrador region in eastern Canada. More than one-third of all guide dogs in North America are Labradors. In England, two-thirds are Labradors.

Many people train Labrador retrievers because they are friendly and faithful to their masters. Labradors are often calmer and gentler than German shepherds.

Labrador retrievers are strong, medium-sized dogs. Most Labradors stand 21.5 to 24.5 inches

(55 to 61 centimeters) tall. They weigh 55 to 80 pounds (25 to 36 kilograms).

Golden Retrievers

Golden retrievers make good guide dogs. They are gentle and strong. They are also easy to train.

People have trained golden retrievers since the 1860s. Golden retrievers first served as gun dogs. Gun dogs find and retrieve animals that are killed by hunters.

Golden retrievers also have the build necessary to be guide dogs. They are 20 to 24 inches (51 to 61 centimeters) tall. They weigh 55 to 75 pounds (25 to 34 kilograms).

Golden retrievers are gentle and strong.

Basic Training

Most guide-dog schools use similar training methods. They have programs for raising guide-dog puppies. Guide-dog puppies must pass basic training before they are guide dogs.

Guide-Dog Puppies

Guide-dog puppies are usually born at guide-dog schools. The puppies leave the schools when they are about two months old. They are placed with foster parents. The puppies become members of the foster families.

Guide-dog schools choose foster parents who can spend a lot of time with puppies. Sometimes the foster parents are adults. But guide-dog schools usually choose children to

Guide dog schools have programs for raising puppies.

be foster parents. Most guide-dog schools require that children be at least nine years old. People who want to help raise guide dogs should contact guide-dog schools near them.

Foster parents have several important tasks. They make sure the guide-dog puppies stay safe. They take the puppies into situations they will face as guide dogs. They might take the puppies into stores or walk them through crowds of people. Foster parents also provide the puppies with food, shelter, and attention.

Guide-dog schools pay the cost of raising the puppies. They pay for all veterinarian care. A veterinarian is a doctor for animals. Foster parents also receive a monthly sum for other expenses like food.

Early Training

Guide dogs start their training while they are still puppies. Their foster parents provide basic obedience training. Obedience training is

Guide dogs start their training as puppies.

Foster parents keep puppies until the puppies are 14 to 18 months old.

teaching an animal to do what it is told. Foster parents also train the puppies to get along with cats and other dogs.

Puppies also learn to obey basic commands during obedience training. Some schools use the commands sit, stay, come, forward, down, stop, leave it, and no. Puppies are ready to train as guide dogs once they know and obey these commands.

Leaving the Foster Parents

Foster parents keep puppies until the puppies are 14 to 18 months old. By then the puppies are fully grown. Then foster parents return the dogs to guide-dog schools for more training.

It is often hard for foster parents to give up the dogs. The foster parents know they may never see the dogs again. Sometimes foster parents present the dogs to their new masters. This happens after the dogs finish their training.

Guide-Dog School

Dogs are assigned to guide-school staff members. These people become the dogs' new handlers. The handlers know that the dogs miss their foster parents. They give dogs extra attention for a few days. The dogs soon make friends with the handlers and adapt to their new homes.

During this time, handlers review obedience training with the dogs. Dogs practice walking beside the handlers, changing directions, and crossing streets. Most dogs learn quickly. They must learn to do their jobs well. If they do not, they could put themselves and their masters in danger.

Advanced Training

Trainers teach the dogs new skills in advanced training. Dogs learn to wear special harnesses. A harness is a set of straps that connects an animal to a person or object. Guide-dog harnesses have handles. These handles allow masters to hold onto the dogs.

Guide dogs learn to respond to the trainers' commands. They learn how to walk in different directions. They change direction based on their trainers' spoken commands.

Dogs learn to wear special harnesses during advanced training.

Trainers also take the guide-dogs through obstacle courses. An obstacle course is a set of objects arranged to test the dogs. Trainers teach the dogs how to guide people around these objects. This prepares the dogs for helping their masters avoid danger.

Guide dogs learn to guide people in many different conditions. First, they learn to guide people in quiet places. Next, they learn to guide people in busy neighborhoods. Finally, the dogs guide people across streets that are filled with cars.

Trainers use praise to help guide dogs learn. The dogs receive generous praise from trainers every time they perform well.

But trainers' praise does not always work. Sometimes trainers have to discipline the dogs. This helps the dogs learn. The dogs repeat tasks if they make mistakes.

Guide dogs learn to guide people across streets.

Guide Dogs and Their Masters

Dogs are not the only ones that need training. The future masters of guide dogs must also receive training. This training is necessary so the dogs and their masters can become teams. Future masters come to the guide-dog schools. They spend about one month learning how to handle their new guide dogs.

Future masters do not meet their guide dogs immediately. First, trainers help them learn how to handle guide dogs. Trainers play the parts of the dogs. They use handles like the ones on dogs' harnesses. The trainers hold one end of the handles. The future masters grip the

Future masters spend about one month learning how to handle their new guide dogs.

other ends. This shows them what to expect when the handles are attached to guide-dog harnesses.

Paired with Guide Dogs

Trainers observe each person's personality during training. Personality is all of the qualities or traits that make one person different from others. Observation helps trainers pick the right dogs for the new masters. Active dogs are paired with active people. Quiet dogs are paired with less active people.

It is an important event when new masters first meet their guide dogs. Each master must get along with the dog right away. First meetings are usually emotional. Dogs and their masters play for a long time and get to know each other. Sometimes masters and the dogs do not get along. Then the masters receive new dogs. The other dogs are assigned to new masters.

It is an important event when new masters first meet their guide dogs.

Team Training

Guide dogs and their new masters must train together to become teams. They must learn to work together and trust each other.

Trainers go everywhere with the new masters and their dogs. Trainers make sure the masters and dogs are able to communicate with each other. The dogs learn their new masters' commands. Trainers make sure the new masters become accustomed to being guided by their dogs.

The trainers test teams in situations that people face on a daily basis. The teams cross busy streets and climb stairs. They go inside grocery stores, banks, and department stores.

Guide dogs also learn when to disobey their masters. For example, dogs refuse to walk in front of cars. The dogs will not put their masters in danger. They will proceed only when it is safe. Their masters know danger

Trainers test teams in situations that people face on a daily basis.

must be present if their guide dogs disobey. The masters praise their dogs for avoiding danger.

Graduation

Some schools have special graduation ceremonies. People celebrate finishing all the required classes at a school. Guide dogs usually graduate when they are about two years old. Masters can graduate at any age.

At graduation, guide-dog schools give the guide dogs to their new masters. Some schools invite the dogs' foster parents to attend the graduation. These foster parents meet the dogs' new masters.

Going Home

Masters take their guide dogs home after completing training. This can be a hard time. At the school, trainers helped the masters with their dogs. At home, there is no one to help.

Some guide dog schools have graduation ceremonies.

Most guide-dog masters become confident soon after returning home. They get more familiar with their guide dogs. They learn that their dogs are eager to please. This helps masters trust their dogs. Before long, masters and their guide dogs travel everywhere together.

Behavior

Sometimes guide dogs misbehave. Sometimes they bark or growl. They might stop to sniff interesting scents. Masters must stop this behavior right away. The dogs will become disobedient if they are allowed to misbehave. They will not pay attention to their work. This could put the masters and the dogs in danger.

Guide-dog schools often send trainers to visit graduates. The trainers check to make sure the dogs and masters are working well together. Sometimes there are no problems. If there are problems, the trainers tell the masters to be patient, consistent, and firm. Dogs change their behavior when they realize their masters will not allow them to misbehave. This helps the dogs and their masters become teams that will work together for many years.

Sometimes guide dogs and their masters have no problems working together.

Stories about Guide Dogs

Guide dogs travel everywhere with their masters. As a result, masters and their guide dogs face dangers together. The dogs may have to think quickly to save themselves and their masters from harm.

Dogs react quickly if their masters fall. Some dogs drag their masters out of danger. Others may bark or cry until help comes.

Guide-dog masters soon learn to trust their dogs' judgment. This trust helps both the dogs and their masters remain safe.

Snow

A snowstorm can affect a guide dog's ability to guide its master. A guide dog named Greta once

A snowstorm can affect a guide dog's ability to guide its master.

faced this problem. A blizzard hid most of the familiar sights. Greta relied upon these sights to guide her master through the neighborhood. She began to paw at the ground and whimper as they approached a bridge.

Greta's master understood the dog's behavior and cleared away as much snow as possible. This helped Greta see the steps leading to the bridge. Greta led her master safely across the bridge.

Fire

One night a fire broke out in a California apartment. A blind musician named Doug lived in the apartment. Doug had a guide dog named Dell.

Dell led Doug down three flights of stairs. Dell guided Doug through smoke and a lot of noise. The local humane society gave Dell a Canine Hero Certificate for saving Doug's life.

Everyday Helpers

There are many more stories about guide dogs. All guide-dog masters can tell stories about

42

Every day, guide dogs help their masters lead safer, busier lives.

how their dogs help them. Every day, the dogs help them lead safer, busier lives.

Dogs work as guides for about eight years before they retire. After they retire, guide dogs live the rest of their lives as family pets. Some masters give their guide dogs back to the foster parents. Other masters give their dogs back to the guide-dog schools. The schools find good homes for the dogs. Masters get new guide dogs.

graduate (GRAJ-oo-ate)—to finish all required classes at a school

harness (HAR-niss)—a set of leather straps connecting an animal to a person or object

obedience training (oh-BEE-dee-uhnss TRAY-ning)—teaching an animal to do what it is told

obstacle course (OB-stuh-kuhl KORSS)—a set of objects arranged to test dogs

personality (pur-suh-NAL-uh-tee)—all of the qualities or traits that make one person different from others

veterinarian (vet-ur-uh-NER-ee-uhn)—a doctor for animals

TO LEARN MORE

Moore, Eva. *Buddy, the First Seeing Eye Dog.* New York: Scholastic, 1996.

Patten, Barbara J. *Dogs With a Job.* Read All About Dogs. Vero Beach, Fla.: Rourke, 1997.

Ring, Elizabeth. *Dogs in Special Service.* Brookfield, Conn.: Millbrook Press, 1994.

Shalant, Phyllis. *The Great Eye.* New York: Dutton's Children's Books, 1996.

To receive the free comic book *Bonnie—The Story of a Seeing Eye Dog*, send your name and address to: The Seeing Eye, Bonnie Book, P.O. Box 375, Morristown, NJ 07963-0375.

USEFUL ADDRESSES

American Council for the Blind
1155 15th Street NW
Suite 720
Washington, DC 20005

Guide Dog Foundation
371 Jericho Turnpike
Smithtown, NY 11787

Guide Dogs for the Blind, Inc.
P.O. Box 151200
San Rafael, CA 94915-1200

The Seeing Eye, Inc.
P.O. Box 375
Morristown, NJ 07960-0375

INTERNET SITES

American Council for the Blind
http://www.acb.org/index.html

Guide Dog Foundation for the Blind, Inc.
http://www.guidedog.org

Guide Dogs for the Blind, Inc.
http://www.guidedogs.com

Guiding Eyes for the Blind
http://www.guiding-eyes.org/

The Seeing Eye Home Page
http://www.seeingeye.org/